lawn of a house just ahead of her a little girl about
five years of age had darted into the roadway. A

NANC
drivi
dark-
some
"It
birth
in hi
He
in th
discu
blue-
Sm
my i
An
lawn
five y
van, t
rel

DREW
home
e con
al pa
s swe
," she
ork."
ther,
home
puzz
l dau
g, Na
tion."
tant l
hous
of ag
ing o
ty f

Her father, Carson Drew, a well-known lawyer in their home town of River Heights, frequently

THIS LETTER BELONGS TO:

Nancy's Mysterious Letter

8

NANCY DREW, an attractive girl of eighteen, was driving home along a country road in her new,

NANCY'S MYSTERIOUS LETTER

by CAROLYN KEENE

awn of a house just ahead of her a little girl about
five years of age had darted into the roadway. A

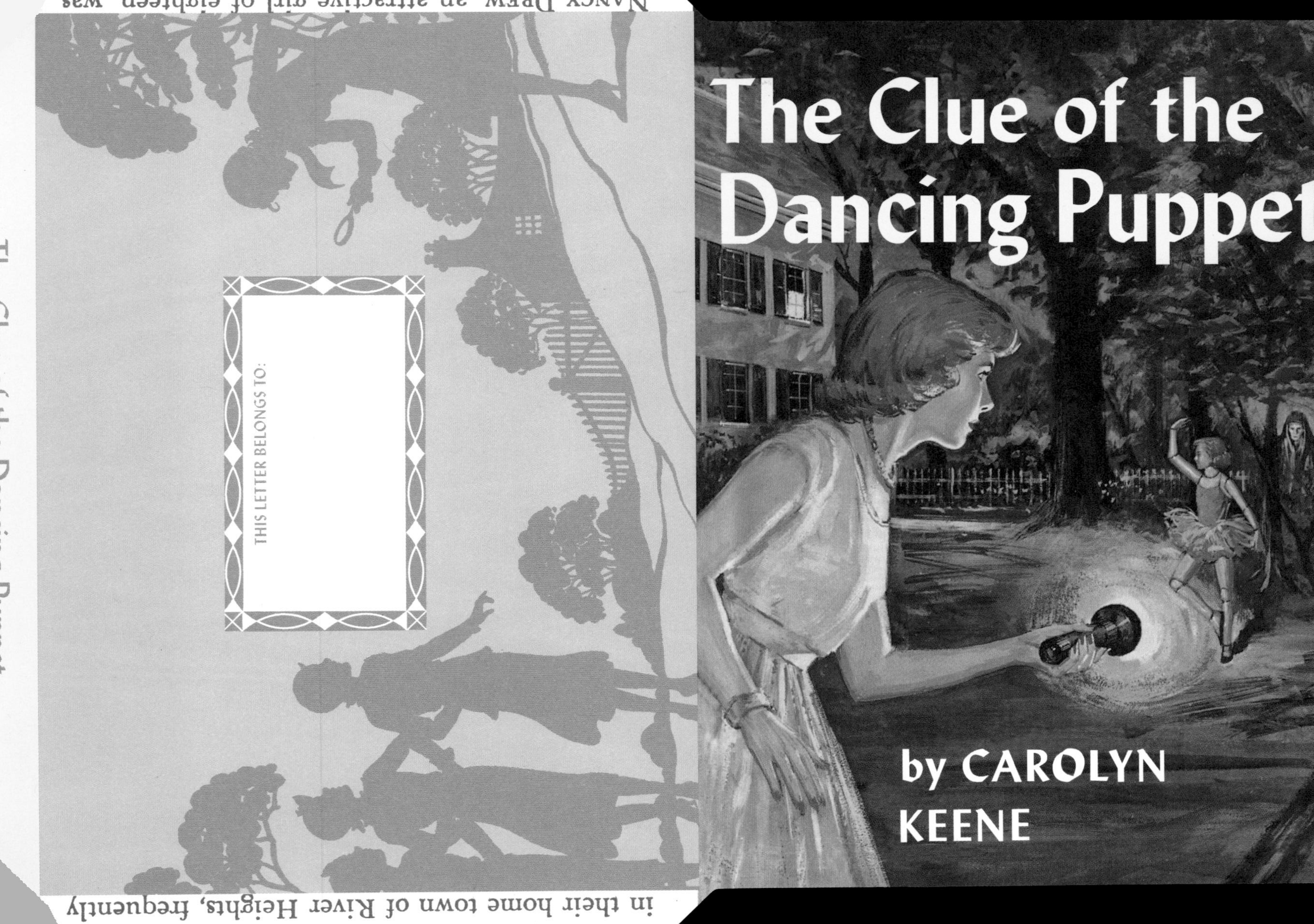
The Clue of the Dancing Puppet
by CAROLYN KEENE
THIS LETTER BELONGS TO:
The Clue of the Dancing Puppet
29
NANCY DREW, an attractive girl of eighteen, was
driving home along a country road in her new
Her father, Carson Drew, a well-known lawyer
in their home town of River Heights, frequently

lawn of a house just ahead of her a little girl about
five years of age had darted into the roadway. A

NANC ... DREW
drivi ... home
dark- ... e con
some ... al pa
"It ... s swe
birth ... ," she
in hi ... ork."
He ... ther,
in th ... home
discu ... puzz
blue- ... l dau
Sm ... g, Na
my i ... tion."
An ... tant k
lawn ... hous
five y ... of ag
van, ... ing o
rel ... ty f

The Clue of the
Whistling Bagpipes
by CAROLYN
KEENE
THIS LETTER BELONGS TO:
NANCY DREW, an attractive girl of eighteen, was
driving home along a country road in her new,
Her father, Carson Drew, a well-known lawyer
in their home town of River Heights, frequently
The Clue of the Whistling Bagpipes
41

lawn of a house just ahead of her a little girl about
five years of age had darted into the roadway. A

NANC
drivi
dark-
some
"It
birth
in hi
He
in th
discu
blue-
Sm
my i
An
lawn
five y
van,
rel

DREW,
home
con
al pa
s swe
," she
ork."
ther,
home
puzz
l dau
g, Na
tion."
tant l
hous
of ag
ing o
ty f

Her father, Carson Drew, a well-known lawyer
in their home town of River Heights, frequently

THIS LETTER BELONGS TO:

The Mystery of the 99 Steps

43

NANCY DREW, an attractive girl of eighteen, was
driving home along a country road in her new,

THE MYSTERY OF THE 99 STEPS

by CAROLYN KEENE

lawn of a house just ahead of her a little girl about
five years of age had darted into the roadway. A

NANC ... DREW
drivi ... home
dark- ... e con
some ... al pa
"It ... s swe
birth ... ," she
in hi ... ork."
He ... ther,
in th ... home
discu ... puzz
blue- ... l dau
Sm ... g, Na
my i ... tion."
An ... tant l
lawn ... hous
five y ... of ag
van, ... ing o
rel ... ty f

THE SPIDER SAPPHIRE MYSTERY

by
Carolyn Keene

THIS LETTER BELONGS TO:

The Spider Sapphire Mystery

45

NANCY DREW, an attractive girl of eighteen, was
driving home along a country road in her new

Her father, Carson Drew, a well-known lawyer
in their home town of River Heights, frequently

lawn of a house just ahead of her a little girl about five years of age had darted into the roadway. A

Her father, Carson Drew, a well-known lawyer
in their home town of River Heights, frequently

THIS LETTER BELONGS TO:

Nancy's Mysterious Letter

8

NANCY DREW, an attractive girl of eighteen, was
driving home along a country road in her new,

NANCY'S MYSTERIOUS LETTER

by CAROLYN KEENE

lawn of a house just ahead of her a little girl about
five years of age had darted into the roadway. A

NANC DREW
drivi home
dark- e con
some al pa
"It s swee
birth ," she
in hi ork."
He ther,
in th home
discu puzz
blue- l dau
Sim g, Na
my i tion."
An tant l
lawn hous
five y s of ag
van, ing o
rel ty f

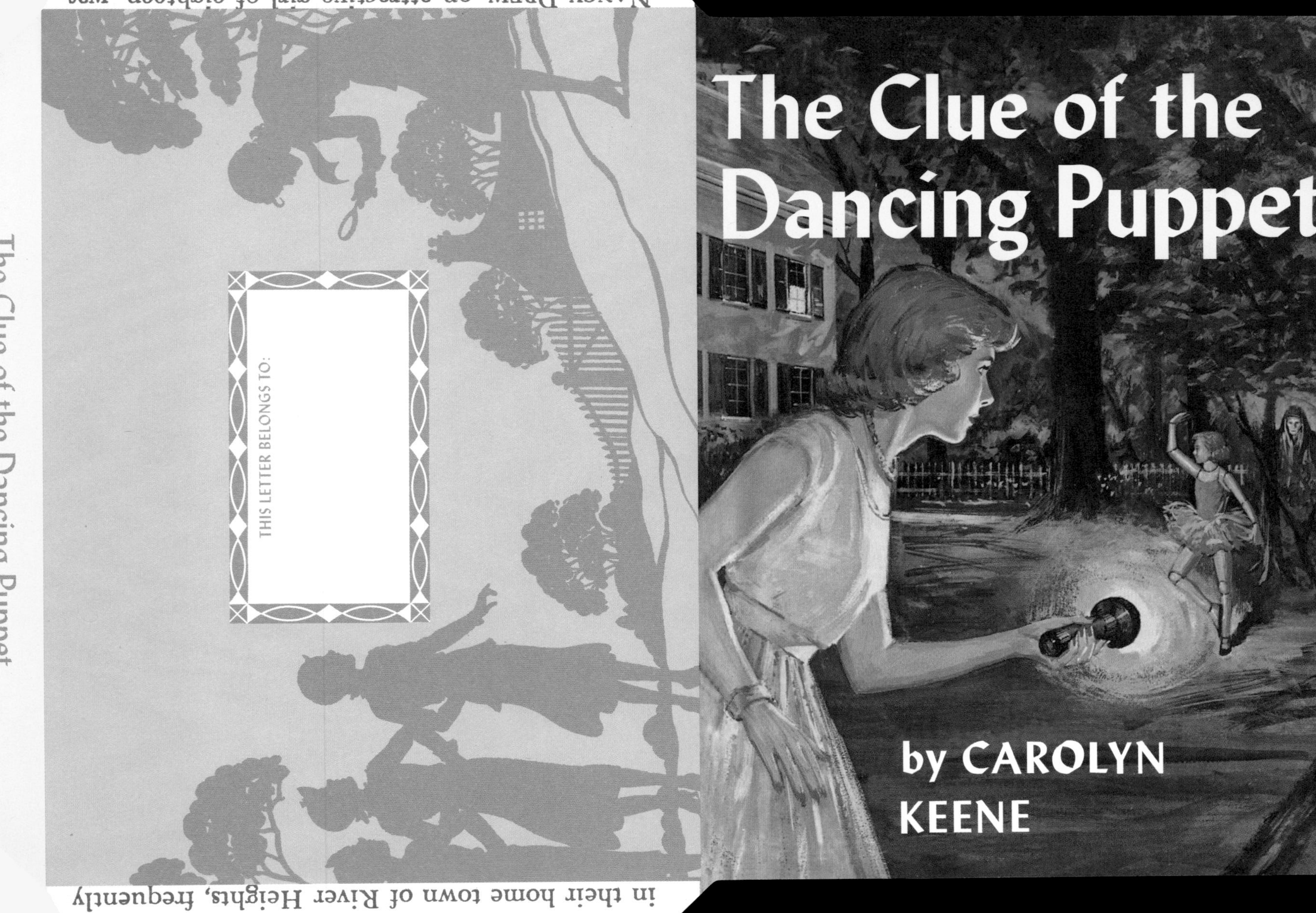
The Clue of the Dancing Puppet
by CAROLYN KEENE
THIS LETTER BELONGS TO:
The Clue of the Dancing Puppet
NANCY DREW, an attractive girl of eighteen, was
driving home along a country road in her new
Her father, Carson Drew, a well-known lawyer
in their home town of River Heights, frequently

lawn of a house just ahead of her a little girl about
five years of age had darted into the roadway. A

NANC … DREW
drivi … home
dark- … con
some … al pa
"It … s swe
birth … ." she
in hi … ork."
He … ther,
in th … home
discu … puzz
blue- … l dau
Sm … g, Na
my i … tion."
An … tant l
lawn … hous
five y … of ag
van, t … ing o
rel … ty f

The Clue of the Whistling Bagpipes

by CAROLYN KEENE

THIS LETTER BELONGS TO:

The Clue of the Whistling Bagpipes

41

NANCY DREW, an attractive girl of eighteen, was driving home along a country road in her new

Her father, Carson Drew, a well-known lawyer in their home town of River Heights, frequently

lawn of a house just ahead of her a little girl about
five years of age had darted into the roadway. A

Her father, Carson Drew, a well-known lawyer in their home town of River Heights, frequently

THIS LETTER BELONGS TO:

NANCY DREW, an attractive girl of eighteen, was driving home along a country road in her new,

THE MYSTERY OF THE 99 STEPS

by CAROLYN KEENE

lawn of a house just ahead of her a little girl about
five years of age had darted into the roadway. A

NANC DREW
drivi home
dark- con
some al pa
"It s swe
birth ," she
in hi ork."
He ther,
in th home
discu puzz
blue- l dau
Sm g, Na
my i tion."
An tant l
lawn hous
five y of ag
van, ing o
rel ty f

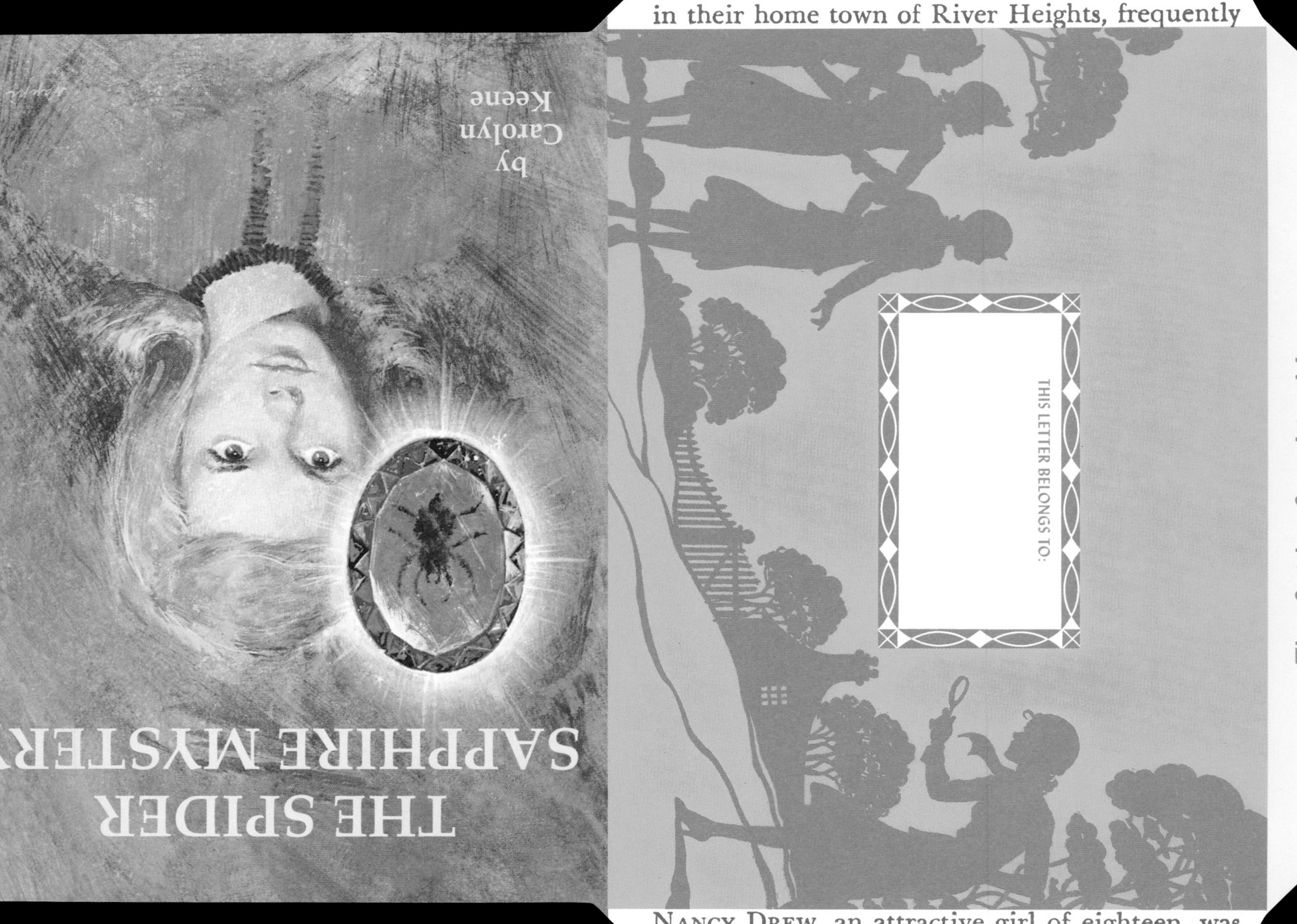

Her father, Carson Drew, a well-known lawyer
in their home town of River Heights, frequently
THIS LETTER BELONGS TO:
The Spider Sapphire Mystery
45
NANCY DREW, an attractive girl of eighteen, was
driving home along a country road in her new
THE SPIDER SAPPHIRE MYSTERY
by Carolyn Keene

lawn of a house just ahead of her a little girl about
five years of age had darted into the roadway. A

NANC ... DREW

drivi ... home
dark- ... e con
some ... al pa
"It ... s swe
birth ... ," she
in hi ... ork."
He ... ther,
in th ... home
discu ... puzz
blue- ... l dau
Si ... g, Na
my i ... tion."
An ... tant l
lawn ... hous
five y ... of a
van, ... ing o
rel ... ty f

Her father, Carson Drew, a well-known lawyer
in their home town of River Heights, frequently

THIS LETTER BELONGS TO:

NANCY DREW, an attractive girl of eighteen, was
driving home along a country road in her new,

NANCY'S MYSTERIOUS LETTER

by CAROLYN KEENE

lawn of a house just ahead of her a little girl about five years of age had darted into the roadway. A

The Clue of the Dancing Puppet

by CAROLYN KEENE

THIS LETTER BELONGS TO:

NANCY DREW, an attractive girl of eighteen, was driving home along a country road in her new,

Her father, Carson Drew, a well-known lawyer in their home town of River Heights, frequently

lawn of a house just ahead of her a little girl about
five years of age had darted into the roadway. A

The Clue of the
Whistling Bagpipes
by CAROLYN
KEENE
THIS LETTER BELONGS TO:
The Clue of the Whistling Bagpipes
41
NANCY DREW, an attractive girl of eighteen, was
driving home along a country road in her new,
Her father, Carson Drew, a well-known lawyer
in their home town of River Heights, frequently

lawn of a house just ahead of her a little girl about five years of age had darted into the roadway. A

Her father, Carson Drew, a well-known lawyer in their home town of River Heights, frequently

THIS LETTER BELONGS TO:

The Mystery of the 99 Steps

43

NANCY DREW, an attractive girl of eighteen, was driving home along a country road in her new,

THE MYSTERY OF THE 99 STEPS

by CAROLYN KEENE

lawn of a house just ahead of her a little girl about
five years of age had darted into the roadway. A

NANC ... DREW
drivi ... home
dark- ... con
some ... al pa
"It ... s swe
birth ... ," she
in hi ... ork."
He ... ther,
in th ... home
discu ... puzz
blue- ... l dau
Sm ... g, Na
my i ... tion."
An ... tant l
lawn ... hous
five y ... of ag
van, ... ing o
rel ... ty f

THE SPIDER SAPPHIRE MYSTERY

by
Carolyn
Keene

THIS LETTER BELONGS TO:

The Spider Sapphire Mystery

45

NANCY DREW, an attractive girl of eighteen, was
driving home along a country road in her new,

Her father, Carson Drew, a well-known lawyer
in their home town of River Heights, frequently

lawn of a house just ahead of her a little girl about
five years of age had darted into the roadway. A

NANC
drivi
dark-
some
"It
birth
in hi
He
in th
discu
blue-
Sm
my i
An
lawn
five y
van,
rel

DREW
iome
: con
al pa
s swe
," she
ork."
ther,
home
puzz
l dau
g, Na
tion.
tant l
hous
of a
ing
ty

Her father, Carson Drew, a well-known lawyer
in their home town of River Heights, frequently

THIS LETTER BELONGS TO:

Nancy's Mysterious Letter

NANCY DREW, an attractive girl of eighteen, was
driving home along a country road in her new,

NANCY'S
MYSTERIOUS
LETTER

by
CAROLYN
KEENE

lawn of a house just ahead of her a little girl about
five years of age had darted into the roadway. A

NANC DREW
drivi home
dark- con
some al pa
"It s swe
birth ," she
in hi ork."
He ther,
in th home
discu puzz
blue- l dau
Sm g, Na
my i tion.
An tant l
lawn hous
five y of ag
van, ing o
rel ty

Her father, Carson Drew, a well-known lawyer
in their home town of River Heights, frequently

THIS LETTER BELONGS TO:

NANCY DREW, an attractive girl of eighteen, was
driving home along a country road in her new,

The Clue of the Dancing Puppet

by CAROLYN KEENE

lawn of a house just ahead of her a little girl about five years of age had darted into the roadway. A

NANC
drivi
dark-
some
“It
birth
in hi
He
in th
discu
blue-
Sm
my i
An
lawn
five y
van, t
rel

DREW
home
e con
al pa
s swe
,” she
ork.”
ther,
home
puzz
l dau
g, Na
tion.
tant l
hous
of ag
ing o
ty f

The Clue of the
Whistling Bagpipes
by CAROLYN
KEENE
THIS LETTER BELONGS TO:
The Clue of the Whistling Bagpipes
41
NANCY DREW, an attractive girl of eighteen, was
driving home along a country road in her new
Her father, Carson Drew, a well-known lawyer
in their home town of River Heights, frequently

lawn of a house just ahead of her a little girl about
five years of age had darted into the roadway. A

NANC | DREW
drivi | home
dark- | con
some | al pa
"It | s swe
birth | ," she
in hi | ork."
He | ther,
in th | home
discu | puzz
blue- | l dau
Sm | g, Na
my i | tion."
An | tant l
lawn | hous
five y | of ag
van, | ing o
rel | ty f

Her father, Carson Drew, a well-known lawyer
in their home town of River Heights, frequently

THIS LETTER BELONGS TO:

The Mystery of the 99 Steps

43

NANCY DREW, an attractive girl of eighteen, was
driving home along a country road in her new,

THE MYSTERY OF THE 99 STEPS

by
CAROLYN
KEENE

lawn of a house just ahead of her a little girl about
five years of age had darted into the roadway. A

NANC | DREW
drivi | home
dark- | con
some | al pa
"It | s swe
birth | ." she
in hi | ork."
He | ther,
in th | home
discu | puzz
blue- | l dau
Sm | g, Na
my i | tion."
An | tant l
lawn | hous
five y | of a
van, | ing o
rel | ty f

Her father, Carson Drew, a well-known lawyer
in their home town of River Heights, frequently

THIS LETTER BELONGS TO:

NANCY DREW, an attractive girl of eighteen, was
driving home along a country road in her new,

The Spider Sapphire Mystery

45

THE SPIDER SAPPHIRE MYSTERY

by Carolyn Keene

lawn of a house just ahead of her a little girl about
five years of age had darted into the roadway. A

NANC … DREW
drivi … home
dark- … con
some … al pa
"It … s swe
birth … ," she
in hi … ork."
He … ther,
in th … home
discu … puzz
blue- … l dau
Sm … g, Na
my i … tion.
An … tant l
lawn … hous
five y … of a
van, … ing
rel … ty

NANCY DREW, an attractive girl of eighteen, was
driving home along a country road in her new,

Nancy's Mysterious Letter

8

THIS LETTER BELONGS TO:

Her father, Carson Drew, a well-known lawyer
in their home town of River Heights, frequently

NANCY'S MYSTERIOUS LETTER

by
CAROLYN
KEENE

lawn of a house just ahead of her a little girl about
five years of age had darted into the roadway. A

The Clue of the Dancing Puppet

by CAROLYN KEENE

THIS LETTER BELONGS TO:

NANCY DREW, an attractive girl of eighteen, was driving home along a country road in her new,

Her father, Carson Drew, a well-known lawyer in their home town of River Heights, frequently

lawn of a house just ahead of her a little girl about
five years of age had darted into the roadway. A

The Clue of the Whistling Bagpipes

by CAROLYN KEENE

THIS LETTER BELONGS TO:

NANCY DREW, an attractive girl of eighteen, was driving home along a country road in her new

Her father, Carson Drew, a well-known lawyer in their home town of River Heights, frequently

lawn of a house just ahead of her a little girl about
five years of age had darted into the roadway. A

NANC ... DREW

drivi ... home
dark- ... con
some ... al pa
"It ... s swe
birth ... ," she
in hi ... ork."
He ... ther,
in th ... home
discu ... puzz
blue- ... d dau
Sm ... g, Na
my i ... tion."
An ... tant l
lawn ... hous
five y ... of a
van, ... ing o
rel ... ty

Her father, Carson Drew, a well-known lawyer
in their home town of River Heights, frequently

THIS LETTER BELONGS TO:

The Mystery of the 99 Steps

43

NANCY DREW, an attractive girl of eighteen, was
driving home along a country road in her new,

THE MYSTERY OF THE 99 STEPS

by CAROLYN KEENE

lawn of a house just ahead of her a little girl about
five years of age had darted into the roadway. A

THE SPIDER SAPPHIRE MYSTERY

by
Carolyn
Keene

THIS LETTER BELONGS TO:

The Spider Sapphire Mystery

45

NANCY DREW, an attractive girl of eighteen, was
driving home along a country road in her new,

Her father, Carson Drew, a well-known lawyer
in their home town of River Heights, frequently

lawn of a house just ahead of her a little girl about
five years of age had darted into the roadway. A

NANC DREW
drivi home
dark- con
some al pa
"It s swe
birth ," she
in hi ork."
He ther,
in th home
discu puzz
blue- d dau
Sim g, Na
my i tion."
An tant l
lawn hous
five y of a
van, ing
rel ty

NANCY'S
MYSTERIOUS
LETTER
by
CAROLYN
KEENE
Drew:
money has been left
Nancy's Mysterious Letter
THIS LETTER BELONGS TO:
Nancy Drew, an attractive girl of eighteen, was
driving home along a country road in her new,
Her father, Carson Drew, a well-known lawyer
in their home town of River Heights, frequently

lawn of a house just ahead of her a little girl about five years of age had darted into the roadway. A

NANC	DREW
drivi	home
dark-	e con
some	al pa
"It	s swee
birth	," she
in hi	ork."
He	ther,
in th	home
discu	puzz
blue-	l dau
Sm	g, Na
my ii	tion.'
An	tant l
lawn	hous
five y	of ag
van,	ing o
rel	ty f

The Clue of the Dancing Puppet

by CAROLYN KEENE

THIS LETTER BELONGS TO:

NANCY DREW, an attractive girl of eighteen, was
driving home along a country road in her new,

Her father, Carson Drew, a well-known lawyer
in their home town of River Heights, frequently

lawn of a house just ahead of her a little girl about
five years of age had darted into the roadway. A

Her father, Carson Drew, a well-known lawyer in their home town of River Heights, frequently

THIS LETTER BELONGS TO:

The Clue of the Whistling Bagpipes

41

NANCY DREW, an attractive girl of eighteen, was driving home along a country road in her new,

The Clue of the Whistling Bagpipes

by CAROLYN KEENE

lawn of a house just ahead of her a little girl about
five years of age had darted into the roadway. A

NANC ... DREW
drivi ... home
dark- ... con
some ... al pa
"It ... s swee
birth ... ," she
in hi ... ork."
He ... ther,
in th ... home
discu ... puzz
blue- ... l dau
Sm ... g, Na
my i ... tion."
An ... tant l
lawn ... hous
five y ... of ag
van, ... ing o
rel ... ty f

THE MYSTERY OF THE 99 STEPS

by
CAROLYN KEENE

THIS LETTER BELONGS TO:

The Mystery of the 99 Steps

NANCY DREW, an attractive girl of eighteen, was driving home along a country road in her new,

Her father, Carson Drew, a well-known lawyer in their home town of River Heights, frequently

lawn of a house just ahead of her a little girl about
five years of age had darted into the roadway. A

THE SPIDER SAPPHIRE MYSTERY

by
Carolyn
Keene

The Spider Sapphire Mystery

45

THIS LETTER BELONGS TO:

NANCY DREW, an attractive girl of eighteen, was
driving home along a country road in her new

Her father, Carson Drew, a well-known lawyer
in their home town of River Heights, frequently

lawn of a house just ahead of her a little girl about five years of age had darted into the roadway. A

NANC
drivi
dark-
some
"It
birth
in hi
He
in th
discu
blue-
Sm
my i
An
lawn
five y
van, t
rel

DREW
home
e con
al pa
s swe
," she
ork."
ther,
home
puzz
l dau
g, Na
tion."
tant l
hous
of ag
ing c
ty f

Her father, Carson Drew, a well-known lawyer
in their home town of River Heights, frequently

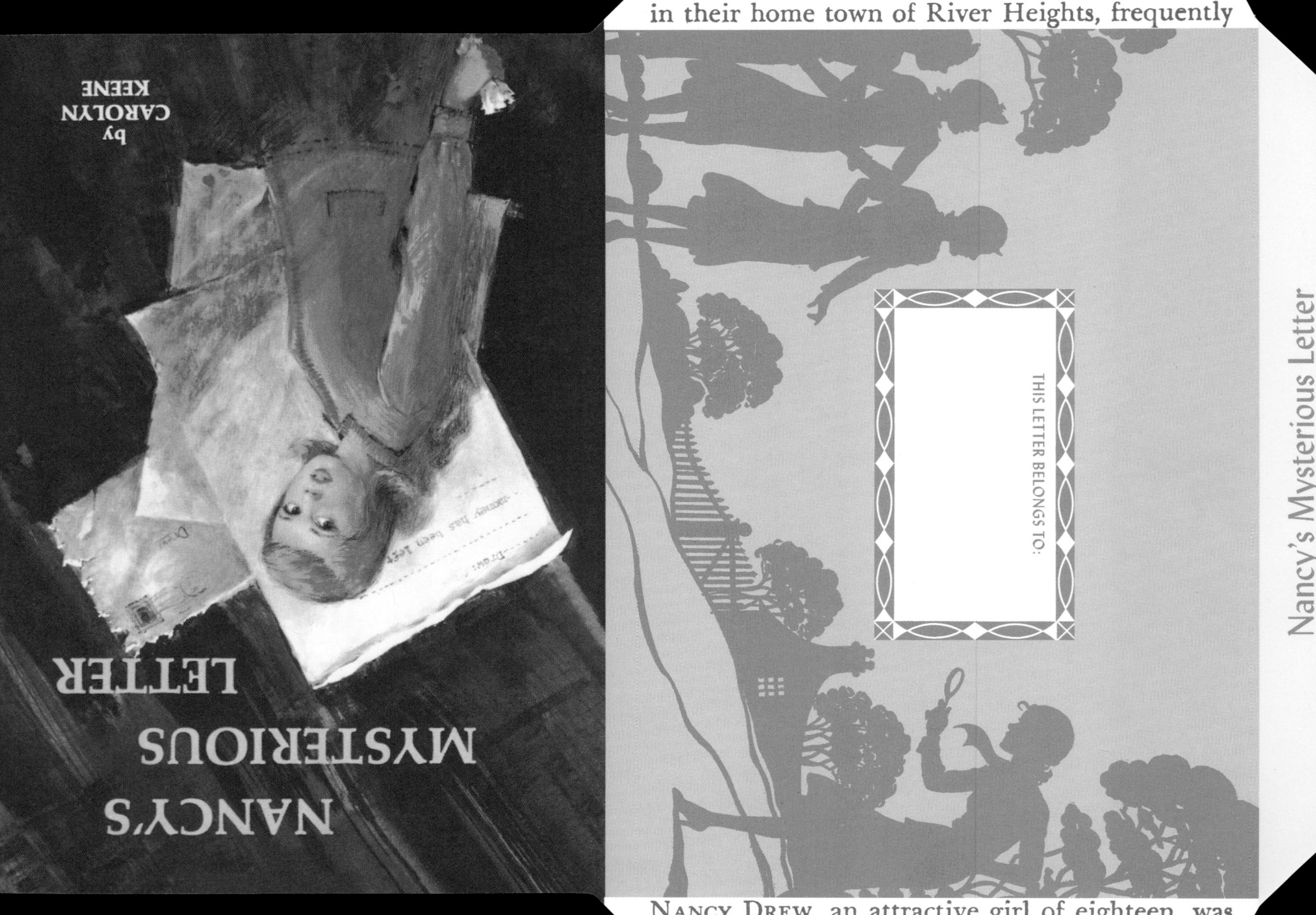

NANCY DREW, an attractive girl of eighteen, was
driving home along a country road in her new,

lawn of a house just ahead of her a little girl about
five years of age had darted into the roadway. A

NANC ... DREW
drivi ... home
dark- ... e con
some ... al pa
"It ... s swe
birth ... ," she
in hi ... ork."
He ... ther,
in th ... home
discu ... puzz
blue- ... l dau
Sim ... g, Na
my i ... tion."
An ... tant l
lawn ... hous
five y ... of ag
van, ... ing o
rel ... ty f

The Clue of the Dancing Puppet

by CAROLYN KEENE

Her father, Carson Drew, a well-known lawyer in their home town of River Heights, frequently

THIS LETTER BELONGS TO:

NANCY DREW, an attractive girl of eighteen, was driving home along a country road in her new,

lawn of a house just ahead of her a little girl about
five years of age had darted into the roadway. A

NANC
drivi
dark-
some
"It
birth
in hi
He
in th
discu
blue-
Sm
my i
An
lawn
five y
van, t
rel

DREW
home
e con
al pa
s swee
," she
ork."
ther,
home
puzz
l dau
g, Na
tion."
tant l
hous
of ag
ing o
ty f

The Clue of the Whistling Bagpipes

by CAROLYN KEENE

NANCY DREW, an attractive girl of eighteen, was driving home along a country road in her new

THIS LETTER BELONGS TO:

The Clue of the Whistling Bagpipes

41

Her father, Carson Drew, a well-known lawyer in their home town of River Heights, frequently

lawn of a house just ahead of her a little girl about
five years of age had darted into the roadway. A

NANC ... DREW
drivi ... home
dark- ... con
some ... al pa
"It ... s swe
birth ... ," she
in hi ... ork."
He ... ther,
in th ... home
discu ... puzz
blue- ... l dau
Sm ... g, Na
my i ... tion."
An ... tant l
lawn ... hous
five y ... of ag
van, ... ing
rel ... ty

Her father, Carson Drew, a well-known lawyer in their home town of River Heights, frequently

THIS LETTER BELONGS TO:

NANCY DREW, an attractive girl of eighteen, was driving home along a country road in her new,

THE MYSTERY OF THE 99 STEPS

by CAROLYN KEENE

lawn of a house just ahead of her a little girl about
five years of age had darted into the roadway. A

NANC ... DREW

drivi ... home
dark- ... e con
some ... al pa
"It ... s swee
birth ... ," she
in hi ... ork."
He ... ther,
in th ... home
discu ... puzz
blue- ... l dau
Sm ... g, Na
my i ... tion."
An ... tant l
lawn ... hous
five y ... of ag
van, ... ing o
rel ... ty f

THE SPIDER SAPPHIRE MYSTERY

by
Carolyn
Keene

THIS LETTER BELONGS TO:

NANCY DREW, an attractive girl of eighteen, was driving home along a country road in her new,

Her father, Carson Drew, a well-known lawyer in their home town of River Heights, frequently

The Spider Sapphire Mystery

lawn of a house just ahead of her a little girl about
five years of age had darted into the roadway. A

NANC ... DREW
drivi ... home
dark- ... con
some ... al pa
"It ... s swe
birth ... ," she
in hi ... ork."
He ... ther,
in th ... home
discu ... puzz
blue- ... l dau
Sm ... g, Na
my i ... tion."
An ... tant l
lawn ... hous
five y ... of a
van, ... ing o
rel ... ty

NANCY'S
MYSTERIOUS
LETTER
by
CAROLYN
KEENE
Nancy's Mysterious Letter
THIS LETTER BELONGS TO:
NANCY DREW, an attractive girl of eighteen, was
driving home along a country road in her new,
Her father, Carson Drew, a well-known lawyer
in their home town of River Heights, frequently

lawn of a house just ahead of her a little girl about
five years of age had darted into the roadway. A

NANC | DREW
drivi | home
dark- | con
some | al pa
"It | s swe
birth | ," she
in hi | ork."
He | ther,
in th | home
discu | puzz
blue- | l dau
Sm | g, Na
my i | tion."
An | tant l
lawn | hous
five y | of a
van, | ing c
rel | ty

The Clue of the Dancing Puppet

by CAROLYN KEENE

THIS LETTER BELONGS TO:

NANCY DREW, an attractive girl of eighteen, was driving home along a country road in her new,

Her father, Carson Drew, a well-known lawyer in their home town of River Heights, frequently

lawn of a house just ahead of her a little girl about
five years of age had darted into the roadway. A

NANC
drivi
dark-
some
"It
birth
in hi
He
in th
discu
blue-
Sm
my i
An
lawn
five y
van, t
rel

DREW
home
e con
al pa
s swe
," she
ork."
ther,
home
puzz
l dau
g, Na
tion."
tant l
hous
of ag
ing o
ty f

The Clue of the Whistling Bagpipes

by CAROLYN KEENE

NANCY DREW, an attractive girl of eighteen, was driving home along a country road in her new,

THIS LETTER BELONGS TO:

Her father, Carson Drew, a well-known lawyer in their home town of River Heights, frequently

The Clue of the Whistling Bagpipes

41

lawn of a house just ahead of her a little girl about
five years of age had darted into the roadway. A

NANC
drivi
dark-
some
"It
birth
in hi
He
in th
discu
blue-
Sm
my i
An
lawn
five y
van, t
rel

DREW
home
e con
al pa
s swee
," she
ork."
ther,
home
puzz
l dau
g, Na
tion."
tant l
hous
of a
ing c
ty f

THE MYSTERY OF THE 99 STEPS

by CAROLYN KEENE

THIS LETTER BELONGS TO:

The Mystery of the 99 Steps

43

NANCY DREW, an attractive girl of eighteen, was driving home along a country road in her new,

Her father, Carson Drew, a well-known lawyer in their home town of River Heights, frequently

lawn of a house just ahead of her a little girl about
five years of age had darted into the roadway. A

THE SPIDER SAPPHIRE MYSTERY

by
Carolyn
Keene

THIS LETTER BELONGS TO:

The Spider Sapphire Mystery

45

NANCY DREW, an attractive girl of eighteen, was
driving home along a country road in her new

Her father, Carson Drew, a well-known lawyer
in their home town of River Heights, frequently